I AM
Who
I AM

I AM *Who* I AM

LELIA WILSON

MILL CITY PRESS

Mill City Press, Inc.
2301 Lucien Way #415
Maitland, FL 32751
407.339.4217
www.millcitypress.net

Unless otherwise indicated, Scripture quotations taken from the King James Version (KJV) – *public domain.*

Paperback ISBN-13: 978-1-6628-4800-1
Ebook ISBN-13: 978-1-6628-4801-8

ACKNOWLEDGEMENTS

I WOULD LIKE TO THANK DR. REV. STAFFORD MILLER FOR HELPING ME TO GET STARTED WRITING THIS BOOK.

I WOULD LIKE TO THANK WALTER AND BETTY MC DANIELS FOR THEIR LOVE, SUPPORT AND WORDS OF ENCOURAGEMENT. I ALSO APPRECIATE THEIR HELP IN GETTING THE BOOK PUBLISHED.

I WOULD ALSO LIKE TO THANK EVERYONE WHO CONTRIBUTED IN ANY WAY TO THE COMPLETION OF THIS BOOK.

DEDICATION

This book is dedicated to my best friend, Patricia Washington, who died February 2, 2021. Thank you for being such a good friend and traveling partner.

OUTLINE

FOREWORD

I wrote this book because I was inspired by the Creator and the times we are living in. I know that there has been many books and studies done on these subjects. What I'm writing about is not new. Some of these subjects have been around since Sodom and Gomorrah. I'm just bringing it up to the 21st century.

As much as things have changed, some things remain the same. The difference in the 21st century is that we have television, computers, internet, cell phones and social media to spread information over the world.

Man is still the dominate factor in all societies and cultures. He does what he wants, when he wants, how he wants, to whom he wants with little or no consequences. Women on the other hand have made great strides in the U.S. especially this year (2021). In other countries, not too much, women are still considered second class citizens. In the U.S. (2021), we have selected our first Black, Indian woman Vice President. More women have been placed in political, social, and business positions than ever before, but we still have a long way to go.

We have many more children being born every day, every year. These children are being exposed to so many factors that affect their sexuality. There are factors in our environment, society, food we eat, water we drink, air we breathe, social media and family that affects a child's sexuality.

I have included a little history, anatomy and physiology, social influences that our children should know about to help them understand themselves. I hope that someone will find this information helpful and interesting.

The Creator made human beings for a reason. Whether you are a male, female, heterosexual, bisexual, homosexual, transgender, etc., the Creator loves you and everyone has a purpose in life.

I AM WHO I AM

I am who I am because GOD made me that way
I am who I am because it seems the only way
I can live my life as I choose to be
I want to be happy, carefree, and free

Life can be hard at times
It makes no sense or rhyme
When one is not comfortable in one
Skin in this day and time

I have to be me
I can't be nobody else
I may not be who you think I should be
I just have to be my self

8/26/19 – YW

PART I

INTRODUCTION

According to the bible, God created the world. Everything in, above, below and around the earth was created by God. This information is found in the Bible, Genesis, chapter one, verses 27-30 (*King James Version*).

When God created man and woman, he did so to procreate the species meaning they would make more people. The same process occurs with animals, plants, fish, birds, and all of God's creation. Each one of us is uniquely made by God. We are all one of a kind.

Males were created differently than females because they are to perform different roles in life. The boy will grow into a man. While he is still young, he will learn how to hunt (according to different societies) for food and later in life learn to take care of the females and children in the family. The father is supposed to teach the male all the skills needed to survive in life. If the father is not present to show the boy how to survive then he will be raised by the village (that may include the mother, grandmother, grandfather, uncles, aunts and sometimes friends). This reference is made to the beginning of time.

As time moves on, the family dynamics change. This can be the result of the dismantling of the family unit due to war, climate, environmental, economic, and social changes.

FAMILY - BASIS OF CILVILIZATION

Cultural and societal effects on families

All cultures, races, ethnic groups, religious organizations, any organization have certain rules that they are governed by. The way people act, dress, look, think, what they eat, how they dance, love, the way they bury their dead, their habits, music, the way they walk, talk, treat people, any traditions are the basis of their existence. These traditions are handed down from generation to generation for thousands of years by way of the family.

Each culture or group is different. The father and/or the mother raises their family according to the way they were raised. Every now and then change happens due to a disaster, traumatic experiences, disease, climate change, war, etc. People must adjust to the situation to survive. We should learn from our past experiences.

The father is usually the head of the family. He is responsible for housing, food, clothing, and all of the essential things needed to survive. In the 21 st century times have changed. Due to the cost of living, it takes both parents to work just to survive. It is very difficult if there is only one parent.

In the year of 2020, the world has come to a stop. People have lost their jobs, homes, businesses, investments, almost everything because of the Corona virus. The government is in turmoil because the president didn't listen to his advisors or scientists. The virus is out of control and over 1,000,000 people have died from the virus.

Before 2020, the family dynamic was changing. In 2017, according to Google, once largely limited to poor women and minorities, single motherhood was becoming the new "norm". This was due in part to the growing trend of children being born outside of marriage - a societal trend that was unheard of decades ago.

About 4 out of 10 children were born to unwed mothers. Nearly two-thirds were born to mothers under the age of 30. Of all single parent families in the U.S., single mothers make up the majority. According to the U.S. Census Bureau, 12 million single parent families in 2016, more than 80% were headed by single mothers. Today 1 in 4 children under the age of 18 - a total of 17.2 million were being raised without a father and almost half (40%) live below the poverty line. For those living with a father only, about 22% live in poverty. In contrast, among the children living with both parents, only 11% were counted as poor.

STATISTICS OF SINGLE PARENT FAMILIES IN THE U.S. IN 2016

83.0 % Single Mother Families

Around 49 % of single mothers have never been married. 51% are either divorced, separated or widowed.

Half have one child, 30% have two. About two thirds are white, one third are black, one quarter are Hispanic. One third have college degrees, while one sixth have not completed high school.

Poverty

Single mothers are more likely to be poorer than married couples. The poverty rate for single mother families in 2015 was 36.5%, nearly five times more than the rate of married couples. More than half (51.9%) lived in extreme poverty with income below half of the federal poverty level - about$9,900 for a family of three. This translates into a weekly family budget of about $200.

Families headed by women of color fared even worse. Nearly two in five (30.9%) of Black females lived in poverty. Hispanic (41.9%), White (30.6%) and Asians (24.2%). Among all other ethnic groups, Native Americans female-headed families with children had the highest poverty rate (48.4%).

Information was obtained from Google-state statistics

PARENTING

I am not a psychologist or a psychiatrist. I am a retired schoolteacher and a college professor of Health and Wellness. Most importantly I am a parent. Being a parent is one of the hardest jobs one can ever have. No one tells you how to be a parent. It's trial and error. Everyone has their own way of doing things. Some people have their parents to help them. Some people read books. The best way to be a parent is hands on experience. You are going to make mistakes. There are a lot of things you do not know. Keep trying until you get it right. To me, the most difficult years of parenting were the years when my children reached puberty. Their bodies and their minds are going through a lot of changes. They become sexually aware and think they know everything.

Parents, be careful of the people who take care of your children. Many parents leave their child or children with a lady in the neighborhood. These people are not trained or licensed to take care of children but do it for the money. Often these people take care of four to five children at one time. These children can be of various ages including infants or toddlers. There are times when older children abuse or mistreat the younger ones. The person in charge cannot be at two places at one time when something happens. If a child can tell the person in charge that they are being abused or hurt, the person in charge will just tell the older child to behave or stop with little or no consequences. If the adult is caring for an infant or toddler (which requires more time and care), then they will not check out the situation. The only way the abuse will stop if the child tells their parent and the parent takes action or finds another person to care for their child or children. Half the time the care giver doesn't even know what has happened.

Parents in poor or minority communities usually look for someone in the neighborhood to care for their child or children because it's cheaper and closer. Most parents find it very expensive to put their child or children in a day care center. They simply can't afford it.

Most parents find people to care for their child or children by word of mouth from other parents or people in the neighborhood. Sometimes it works and sometimes it doesn't.

Abuse can go on for a long time if the child is too young to tell what is happening to them. What is a parent to do if they work and don't know how to check out a person? Check your child for marks and bruises. Talk to your child and most importantly, listen to them. A child who suffers abuse can be traumatized for life.

Many parents will not be accepting of the changes in attitude and actions. This is a crucial time when communication is most important. That is why one has to talk to their children. Children will be influenced by their environment and peers. If you give them a solid foundation of love, religion and discipline, you might have children that turn out alright. There are no guarantees.

The government passed a law forbidding physical discipline in raising children. As a result, children have gotten out of control. They are disrespectful to everyone. They curse and even fight their parents. Children tell their parents what to do and many parents are afraid of their own children.

Discipline is a very important part of raising children (as long as it is not abusive to the extent of physical or mental harm).I once heard that if you spare the rod, you spoil the child. Discipline helps the child to respect their parents and others, know the boundaries as to what is right or wrong and to know what they can and cannot do.

This law has created monsters and society does not know how to correct this situation. If the government cannot run the government efficiently, how can they tell families how to raise their children? These are my personal thoughts.

I AM A MALE

ROLE OF A MALE IN THE UNITED STATES

When we talk about the role of a male in the United States, we must go back to the beginning of his life. When a male child is born, he is placed into a world where everything is based on his gender. His role is based upon his family, culture and his environment. The gender role comes through our parents, male relatives, teachers and peers. We are acclimated into these roles starting in infancy.

The boy's room would be painted blue, he would be wearing boy's clothes and playing with boy toys such as cars, trucks, soldiers, and guns. They are told that they have to be tough, rough, self-reliant, not showing emotions ("a man is not supposed to cry") not to act like a girl.

A man's behavior, attitudes are passed down from generation to generation. The word Masculinity as defined by Wikipedia (also called manhood and manliness) is a set of attributes, behavior and roles associated with men and boys. The roles

11

and behavior learned by a person as determined by their sex is determined by a person's cultural norms. The gender role means how they are to act, how they speak, dress, groom and conduct themselves based their assigned sex.

Children learn at an early age to discriminate certain behaviors by the way they are treated by their family, friends, teachers, members of the community, etc. As a boy grows older, many men follow in the steps of their fathers in terms of employment and education. Many industries that once were the source of income in many areas of the country have changed, such as mining, steel industry, and the auto industry. Once these jobs shut down, many men and women lost their source of income and their livelihood. Many men had to move away to areas where they could find work.

Some men resort to playboy behavior, power over women and self-reliance. The man is the one who can fertilize a female's egg, thus producing another life.

Some men are seen as an aggressor, risk takers, work oriented, assertive, rational, bold, strong, fearless, courageous, a provider and protector.

Although sexuality is commonly represented in advertising and other media as having to do solely with physical gratification, most people are aware how sexuality involves much more than the stimulation of the body sex organs. Sexuality has several dimensions including the following:

Sexuality: The physical dimension

One of the fundamental functions of sexuality is biological reproduction. Males produce the sperm and deposit them in the female reproductive tract during sexual intercourse. Females provide capable eggs, called ova and a safe nutrient filled environment in which the fetus develops for the 9 months of pregnancy.

Males are created differently than females because they are to perform different roles in life. The boy will grow into a man and would learn how to do different things. Long ago the boy would learn how to hunt for food and to take care of the female. The father is supposed to teach the males all the skills needed to survive in life. If the father is not present in the boy's life to show him how to survive, then he will be raised by "the village". Remember, we all have to answer to the Creator in the end.

Also in Eldin' s and Gladin book on Health and Wellness (10th edition), it is stated that the male and female sexual biology's are genetically determined at conception. The fusion of an x bearing egg with the x bearing sperm produces a female (XX). The fusion with a bearing sperm produces a male (XY).

Once the chromosome pattern is set, the development of the sexual anatomy follows the precise instructions of the genes contained in the chromosomes. A particular chromosome set determines whether the as-yet immature sex cells that appear around the fifth week of development will eventually produce a sperm or an ova.

The sex chromosomes determine whether the fetus will ultimately develop the male sex organs (testes, sperm ducts, semen producing glands, and penis).

The American Academy of Pediatrics does not recommend routine neonatal circumcision (the American Academy of pediatrics, 2005). Removal of the foreskin does eliminate the buildup of **smegma**, a white, cheesy substance that can accumulate under the foreskin.

Male sexual anatomy consists of two testes, the sites of sperm and sex hormone production; a series of connected sperm ducts that originated at the testes, course through the pelvis and terminates at the urethra of the penis; glands that produce seminal fluid; and the penis.

The testes are in a flash covered sac, the scrotum, that hangs outside the man's body. In the embryo, the testes develop inside the body but just before birth they descend into the scrotum. Inside the scrotum, the testes are kept at a temperature a few degrees cooler than the internal body temperature, a condition necessary to produce reproductively capable sperms. Normally, the scrotum hangs loosely from the body's wall, although cool or cold temperatures, fear, excitement, or sexual stimulation may cause it to move closer to the body. One testis is usually a little higher than the other.

When a man ejaculates, sperm are propelled through the sperm duct and out of the penis by contractions of the smooth muscle that lines the sperm ducts and the muscles of the pelvis. As they move out of the body, the sperm mixes with secretions of seminal fluid from the seminal vesicles, prostate gland, and Cowper's glands to form semen. The semen, which is the gelatinous milky fluid emitted at ejaculation, contains a mixture of about 300 million sperm cells in about 3 to 6 milliliters of seminal fluid. The seminal fluid contributes 95% or more of the entire volume of semen.

The penis is normally soft, but when a man becomes sexually aroused, its internal tissues will fill with blood and the penis enlarges and becomes erect. All men are born with a fold of skin, the foreskin, that covers the end of the penis.

In the United States today, parents of male infants can elect to have the foreskin removed surgically within hours after a child's birth. Removal of the foreskin is called **circumcision**. Muslims and Jewish traditions call for the circumcisions of all males. Although circumcision may lessen the risk of adult penile cancer and at circumcision leads to an increase in sexual arousal because it exposes the glands, and the related belief that circumcision produces an inability to delay ejaculation, are myths. For most men, circumcision has no effect on sexual arousal and sexual activity.

The basic difference between a boy and a girl is the genitals (private parts). The boy has a penis on the outside of his body and the girls' private parts are on the inside of her body. The male's body will change as he gets older or reaches puberty. Puberty is that time in life when a boy or girl can procreate or have children.

According to Edlin and Golanty book on Health and Wellness 1 (tenth edition)" Sexuality involves the simultaneous expression of mind, body and spirit - the whole self. In today's society, sexuality is represented in advertising and other media as having to do solely with physical gratification, most people are aware that sexuality involves much more than stimulation of the body's sex organs.

Sexuality has several dimensions:

1. The physical dimension: those parts of the body that defines a person as female or male, contributes to sexual experiences and are involved in reproduction.
2. The psychological dimension: values, beliefs, attitudes and emotions that influences a person's sexual thoughts and behavior.
3. The orientation dimension: the tendency to feel attracted to and desire to emotionally bond with a member of the same or other sex.
4. The behavioral dimension: physical and social activities intended to meet one's sexual wants and needs.
5. The relationship dimension: aspects of sexuality that interface and integrate with intimate relationships from the standpoint of personal health. Sexuality is an area over which you have considerable individual control. You choose when and with whom you wish to have sex

and which feelings you wish to express in sexual ways. With some fundamental knowledge of sexual biology, you can conduct your sexual life responsibly thus avoiding unnecessary illness and exercising a choice of whether and when to have children.

Male and female sexual biology are genetically determined at conception. The fusion of the X-bearing egg with the X-bearing sperm produces a female (XX). Fusion with the Y-bearing sperm produces a male (XY). Once the chromosome pattern is set, the development of the sexual anatomy follows from the precise instructions of the genes contained in the chromosomes. A particular chromosome set determines whether the immature sex cells that appear at about the fifth week of development will eventually produce sperm or ova.

The sex chromosomes determine whether the fetus will ultimately develop the male sex organs-testes, sperm ducts, semen-producing glands and penis - or the female organs - ovaries, fallopian tubes, uterus, vagina, and the external female genitals.

The genetic determination of sexual biology also specifies the pattern of male or female steroid hormone production, which in turn affects the secondary sex characteristics that distinguish male and female: the extent and distribution of facial and body hair; body build and stature; and appearance of breasts.

Sexually: The Psychological Dimension

The psychological dimension of sexuality consists of one's emotions - most frequently joy, excitement, pleasure, love and affection - and the conscious and unconscious beliefs that guide the interpretation of experience and generate behaviors designed to meet one's sexual and relationship needs.

These Include an assessment of one's social and sexual attractiveness, one's self-worth, and appropriate attitudes and behaviors for members of each sex (gender roles).

They also include beliefs about what is "natural", beautiful, good, the behaviors considered "proper" for sexual activity, when and where sexual activity may take place and who may legitimately have sex with whom. Some beliefs area specific to an individual, such as the willingness to engage in "casual sex", and others are shared among a group, such the disapproval of having sexual relationships with someone other than one's spouse. Occasionally a society's shared beliefs are codified into law, such as the prohibition of prostitution.

Beliefs are acquired through socialization, the process by which a social group confers attitudes and behavioral expectations upon individuals. It is through socialization that individuals learn what sexuality means for members of their group. Socializing influences include parents, family, school, peer groups, religion, employment setting and mass media.

Sexuality: The Orientation Dimension

About 50% of the population have had some same-sex sexual experience, often occurring in childhood and adolescence when sexual experimentation is common. Many people say they are erotically aroused by individuals of their sex but have no desire to act on those feelings. Traditionally our culture has forbidden same-sex sexual and intimate relationships, asserting that they are wrong Sexual orientation is the propensity to be sexually and romantically attracted to members of a particular sex. People with a same-sex orientation area referred to as homosexuals; people with an other-sex orientation are referred to as Heterosexual. People whose orientation is for either sex is referred to as Bisexual. It is estimated that 5% to 10% of adults are exclusively homosexual. Some surveys indicated that, immoral, unnatural, or indicative of psychological illness.

Neither the American Psychological Association nor the American Psychiatric Association considers same-sex orientation to be a mental illness. Scientific studies have failed to uncover any inherited, hormonal, or metabolic abnormalities that account for same-sex orientation. The neuropsychological mechanisms underlying the development and patterning of sexual orientation are unknown. One thing that is certain is that sexual orientation is rarely a choice, to everyone, it seems "natural".

By and large, same-sex intimate relationships are like other-sex ones, with the possible exception that they involve less gender-specific stereotypical behaviors. Some same-sex relationships are casual and do not involve long –term commitments, whereas others involve a deep and lasting commitment and sexual exclusivity. Sexual orientation does not affect the desire to love and to be loved and to be involved in committed, caring relationships.

I AM A FEMALE

THE ROLE OF THE FEMALE

From the time a female is born, she is introduced into a world of femininity. She will wear pretty dresses, wear bows and ribbon in her hair, play with dolls, doll houses, have dishes and tea pots, and is adorned with frilly things. The gender roles are based on norms and standards set by society.

Masculine roles are usually associated with strength, aggression, and dominance. Female roles are associated with passivity, nurturing and subordination. The role of a female is usually one of a caretaker, mother, educator, farmer, entrepreneur, cook, house keeper and keeper of the family.

Throughout history, the central role of the woman in society has been to insure the stability, progress, and long-term development of the family. Women are the primary caretakers of children and elders in every country of the world. They are likely to be the person to make whatever changes that need to be made concerning the family. A woman is a man's helpmate, partner, comrade, and the mother of his children. She sacrifices her personal pleasures as an administrator and leader of the household.

Women were considered second class citizens from the mid-18th century to the mid-19th century. They started a feminist movement to defend a state of equal political, economic, cultural freedom for women. They wanted to be free to vote and do the things they wanted to do and not be under the rule of men. Women were portrayed to be responsible for tending to the house, raising of the children, and looking after their husbands. Roles have changed since then due to TV, the phone, advertisements, and social media.

This is a new day and new time for women. Jobs that once were considered men's jobs are being done by women (politicians, factory workers, miners, astronauts, military, auto industry, police, F.B.I. and every area of the government). Women are proving that they are an important part of society. This is indeed a new day for women.

The role of a female is to take care of the family and to reproduce. The female usually learns what to do from her mother or grandmother. Sometimes she must learn on her own if the mother or grandmother is unable to do so.

The physical dimensions of sexuality - Female Anatomy

(Information was obtained from Eldin and Gladin 's book, Health and Wellness, 10th edition)

A woman's internal sexual organs consist of **two ovaries**, which lie on either side of the abdominal cavity, **the fallopian tubes, the uterus**, and **the vagina**; together these structures make up a specialized tube that goes from each ovary to the outside of the body. The function of the ovaries, which are about the size and shape of almonds, is to produce fertilizable ova as well as sex hormones, which control the development of the female body type, maintain normal female sexual physiology and help regulate the course of pregnancy. The fallopian tubes gather and transport the ova that are released from the ovaries (about one each month). The two fallopian tubes connect to the uterus, an organ about the size of a woman's fist, which is sitting just behind the pelvic bone and the bladder. The uterus is part of the passageway for the sperm as they move from the vagina to the fallopian tubes to effect fertilization; after fertilization, it provides the environment in which the fetus grows. It is the inner lining of the uterus that is shed each month in menstruation.

The lower part of the uterus is the **cervix**, and the cavity of the uterus is connected to the vagina by means of a small opening called the cervical os. The cervix secretes mucus, which changes in consistency depending on the phase of the menstrual cycle. Some women learn to estimate the time of ovulation (ovum release) by examining their cervical mucus.

The vagina is a hollow tube that leads from the cervix to the outside of the body. The sexually non-aroused vagina is approximately 3 to 5 inches long. Normally, the vaginal tube is rather narrow, but it can readily widen to accommodate the penis during intercourse, a tampon during menstruation, the passage of a baby during childbirth or a pelvic examination. The vagina possesses a unique physiology that is maintained by the secretions that continually emanate from the vagina walls. These secretions help regulate the growth of micro-organisms that normally inhabit the vagina and they also help to cleanse the vagina. Because the vagina is a self-cleaning organ, it is usually unnecessary to employ any extraordinary cleaning measures, such as douching. Very often douching merely upsets the natural chemical balance of the vagina and increases the risk of developing vaginal inflammation called **vulvovaginitis** or **vaginitis**. Symptoms of vulvovaginitis include irritation or itching, redness or swelling of the vagina and vulva, unusual discharge, discomfort or a burning sensation when urinating and sometimes a disagreeable odor.

Vulvovaginitis is commonly referred to as a "yeast infection". Whereas yeast (typically Candida albicans) can cause vulvovaginitis, other microorganisms, such as the protozoan Trichomonas vaginalis, bacteria and viruses, also cause it. Even irritation from vaginal sprays, spermicidal products and other chemicals can produce symptoms of vulvovaginitis. Anyone with symptoms of vulvovaginitis should see a health practitioner to obtain an accurate diagnosis and treatment.

A number of factors increase susceptibility to vulvovaginitis including the use of antibiotics, emotional stress, a diet high in carbohydrates, hormonal changes caused by pregnancy or birth control pills, chemical irritants, intercourse without adequate lubrication and heat and moisture retained by nylon underwear and pantyhose.

The vulva encompasses all female external genital structures- pubic hair, the folds of skin, the **clitoris** and the urinary and vaginal openings. The smaller, inner pair of folds are called the **labia minora**, and the larger, outer pair are called the **labia majora**. The **clitoris**, a highly sensitive sexual organ, is situated above the vaginal opening.

The opening of the **urethra**, which is the exit tube for urine, is located at the vaginal region just below the clitoris. The fact that the urethra is only about the one –half an inch long and located close to the vagina makes it susceptible to irritation and infection, called **urethritis**, characterized by a burning sensation during urination and usually by the frequent urge to urinate. Occasionally, bacteria introduced into the urethra migrate the short distance to the bladder and produce a bladder infection called **Cystitis**. The symptoms of cystitis are like those of urethritis. The occurrence of urethritis or cystitis is often referred to as a **urinary tract infection or UTI**.

The most frequent causes of a UTI are irritation from sexual intercourse and the introduction of bacteria (principally **E.Coli**) from the anal region into the vaginal region and into the urethra. To prevent UTIs care should be taken not to introduce anal bacteria into the vaginal region during sexual activity (manually or with the penis). It is recommended that a woman urinate immediately after having sex, wear absorbent cotton underpants or underpants with cotton crotch and wipe the urethra in the front to back direction after urinating.

The risk of urethritis or cystitis can be lessened by drinking a lot of fluids to wash the bacteria from the urinary tract and by drinking cranberry juice to prevent bacteria from clinging to the cells lining the urinary tract. If a UTI occurs, it is advisable not to drink alcohol or ingest caffeine or spices, for these substances may irritate an already inflamed urinary tract. If pain is severe or if there is blood in the urine, consult a physician. UTIs can be successfully treated with medications.

The breast consists of a network of milk glands and milk ducts embedded in fatty tissue and are affected by pregnancy, nursing, or birth control pills, as well as the different phases of the menstrual cycle. The variation in breast size among women is due to differing amounts of fatty tissue within the breast. There is little variation among women in the amount of milk –producing tissue; thus, a woman's ability to breastfeed is unrelated to the size of her breasts.

Menstrual Cycle

Approximately monthly, a woman usually produces a single ovum that can be fertilized. These periods of ovum production are referred to as the woman's fertility cycle. During the **fertility cycle**, a woman's body undergoes several hormonal induced changes to prepare her body for pregnancy. One of these changes is the thickening of the lining of the uterus, the **endometrium**, to support the first stages of pregnancy. In addition, special blood vessels in the uterus increase in size. Their role is to bring maternal nutrients to the embryo and later in pregnancy, to the fetus. If conception does not occur, the endometrium and the special blood vessels are sloughed off and leaves the body via the vagina. This is **menstruation**. Between 15 to 45 million liters (about 2 to 3 teaspoons) of material are discharged over the span of three to six days. The length of time from one menstruation to another is the **menstrual cycle**.

The length and regularity of the menstrual cycle vary from woman to woman. Most women experience cycles of approximately 28 days, with cycle lengths between 24 and 35 days being the most common. Shorter and longer cycles are possible.

For some women, menstruation may be accompanied by unpleasant symptoms. It is estimated that half of women experience abdominal pain, commonly referred to as "**cramps**" and medically referred to as **dysmenorrhea**, usually during the first day or so of menstruation. Another menstrual difficulty is change in feelings and disposition as the time of menstruation approaches and during the first day or two of menstrual flow. These symptoms may include headache, backache, fatigue, feeling bloated, breast tenderness, depression, irritability, unusual aggressive feelings and social withdrawal.

Another common menstrual difficulty is amenorrhea, defined as the interruption or cessation of regular menstrual periods.

Menopause

Menarche is the first menstruation a young woman experience. The average age for a girl is between 12 and 13 years, although it can occur as early as 9 years or as late as 19 years. Menopause is the gradual cessation of ovulation and menstruation. The two principal biological consequences of menopause are that a woman no longer can become pregnant and that her body may undergo changes from the diminished production of estrogen. Many women experience menopause between the ages 50 and 52; however, it can occur as early as 35 and as late as 55. The age at which menopause occurs may be affected by hereditary, social, and nutritional factors. There is no relation between the age at which menopause occurs and the age at which a woman first begins to menstruate.

SEXUALITY: THE PSYCHOLOGICAL DIMENSION

The psychological dimension of sexuality consists of one's emotions - most frequently joy, excitement, pleasure, love, and affection - the conscious and unconscious belief that guide the interpretation of experience and generate behaviors designed to meet on sexual and relationship needs. These include an sex assessment of one social and sexual attractiveness, one's self-worth and appropriate attitudes and behaviors for members of each sex (gender roles).

They also include beliefs about what is "natural", beautiful, and good, the behaviors considered " proper" for sexual activity, where sexual activity may take place and who may legitimately have sex with whom. Some beliefs are specific to an individual, such as willingness to engage in quote "casual", and others shared among a group, such as the disapproval of having sexual relations with someone other than one's spouse. Occasionally a society's shared beliefs are codified into law, such as the prohibition of prostitution.

Beliefs are acquired through socialization, the process by which a social group confers attitudes and behavioral expectations upon individuals. It is through socialization that individuals learn what sexuality means for members of their group. Socializing influences include parents, family, school, peer groups, religion, employment settings, and mass media.

The sociological aspect of being a man or woman

We are products of our environments. It takes a man to show a boy how to be a man. I must rephrase that by saying a good man. It takes a good man to show a boy how to be a good man. There are many men that are not good men, and they don't know how to be a good man because they have never been around a good man.

It takes a good woman to show a girl how to be a good woman. A man cannot show a girl how to be a woman because he is not a woman.

If a man or a woman did not have a positive role model growing up in life, then he or she cannot pass on positive traits to their children. Children will mimic whatever they see around them.

As times move on, the family dynamics change. This can be the result of the dismantling of the family unit due to war, climate, environmental changes, economic and social changes. At this time (2021), according to Google, once largely limited to poor women and minorities, single motherhood is becoming the new "norm". This is due in part to the growing trend of children being born outside of marriage-a societal trend that was unheard of decades ago.

PART II

HOMOSEXUALITY IN THE BIBLE

Almost every life's situation can be founded in the bible, homosexuality is no exception. In the King James' Version, Genesis 19: 1-29, we find a whole city being destroyed because of their sinful ways.

Chapter 19-1 – And there came two angels to Sodom at even; and Lot sat in the gate of Sodom: and Lot seeing them rose up to meet them; and he bowed himself with his face toward the ground.

2 And he said, "Behold now, my lords, turn in, I pray you, into your servant's house, and tarry all night, and wash your feet and ye shall rise up early and go on your ways." And they said, "But we will abide in the street all night."

3 And he pressed upon them greatly; and they turned in unto him and entered his house; and he made them a feast and did bake unleavened bread and they did eat.

4 But before they lay down, the men of the city, even the men of Sodom, compassed the house round, both old and young, all the people from every quarter:

5 And they called unto Lot and said unto him, "Where are the men who came into thee this night? Bring them out unto us, that we may know them."

6. And Lot went out at the door unto them and shut the door after him.

7 And said, "I pray you, brethren, do not so wickedly."

8 "Behold now, I have two daughters which have not known man; let me, I pray you, bring them out unto you and do ye to them as is good in your eyes; only unto these men do nothing; for therefore came they under the shadow of my roof."

9 And they said, "Stand back, this one fellow came into sojourn, and he will needs be a judge; now will we deal worse with thee, than with them." And they pressed sore upon the man, even Lot and came near to break the door.

10 But the men put forth their hand and pulled Lot into the house to them and shut the door.

11. And they smote the men that were at the door of the house with blindness, both small and great: so that they wearied themselves to find the door.

12 And the men said unto Lot, "Hast thou here any besides? Son in law and thy sons, and they daughters and whatsoever thou hast in the city, bring them out of this place:

13 For we will destroy this place, because the cry of them waxen great before the face of the Lord; and the Lord hath sent us to destroy it."

14 And Lot went out, and spoke unto his sons in law, which married their daughters, and said "Up, get out of this place; for the Lord will destroy this city. But he seemed as one that mocked unto his sons in law."

15 And when the morning arose, then the angels hastened Lot, saying, "Arise, take thy wife and thy two daughters, which are here; lest thou be consumed in the iniquity of the city."

16 And while he lingered, the men laid hold upon his hand and upon the hand of his wife and upon the hand of his two daughters; the Lord being merciful unto him: and they brought him forth and set him without the city.

17 And it came to pass, when they had brought them forth abroad, that he said, "Escape for thy life; look not behind thee, neither stay thou in all the plain; escape to the mountain, lest thou be consumed."

18 And Lot said unto them, "Oh, not so, my Lord:

19 Behold now, thy servant hath found grace in thy sight and thou hast magnified thy mercy, which thou hast shewed unto me in saving my life; and I cannot escape to the mountain, lest some evil take me, and I die."

20 Behold now, this city is near to flee unto and it is a little one: Oh, let me escape thither, (Is it not a little one?) and my soul shall live.

21 And he said unto him, "See, I have accepted thee concerning this thing also, that I will not overthrow this city, for the which thou has spoken.

22. Haste thee, escape thither; for I cannot do anything till thou become thither." Therefore, the name of the city was called Zoar.

23 The sun was risen upon the earth when Lot entered Zoar.

24 Then the Lord rained upon Sodom and upon Gomorrah brimstone and fire from the Lord out of heaven;

25 And he overthrew those cities and all the plain and all the inhabitants of the cities and that which grew upon the ground.

26 But his wife looked back from behind him, and she became a pillar of salt.

27 And Abraham got up early in the morning to the place where he stood before the Lord:

28 And he looked toward Sodom and Gomorrah and toward all the land of the plain, and beheld, and lo, the smoke of the country went up as the smoke of a furnace.

29 And it came to pass, when God destroyed the cities of the plain, that God remembered Abraham and sent Lot out of the midst of the overthrow, when he overthrew the cities in which Lot dwelt.

MY INTERVIEW WITH A HOMOSEXUAL

In my many years of life, I have met many people of all gender differences. I've tried to treat all people the way I wanted to be treated. As a professional dancer I've worked with many dancers who were homosexual or lesbians (they might have been bisexual because they married heterosexual men) . They were like my brothers or sisters. As a teacher of dance, I had many students who were homosexuals and were very talented. I had some female students who were lesbians. If they respected me, I respected them.

I had one student who was homosexual, who I trusted and supported. He stole the keys to my home and my car when we were rehearsing for a show. I had no idea that he was the one until the police arrested him driving my car on the expressway. Naturally I pressed charges and he went to jail. I think he took my kindness for weakness. I never thought that he would do something like that to me. I think he had mental issues.

While writing this book, I asked several people who I knew who had gender differences to tell me about their experiences. Most of them declined. Only one agreed to share his story.

This is his story:

Interview Questions

1. What sex were you born? answer*: male*
2. What is your race? answer*: Hispanic*
3. What is your sexual orientation now? answer: *homosexual*
4. What is your age now (2019)? answer: 43
5. At what age did you know that you were different sexually? answer*: 6 years old*
6. Did any incident happen to you when you were young that might have affected your sexual orientation? Explain: *I always knew that I was different. I was attracted to boys. At the age of 7, I had sexual intercourse with a 15 year old boy who was my cousin's best friend. At that time, I thought it was the normal thing to do. As I grew older and experienced sex with other men, I still had the same feelings. The only thing I regret is that I started at such an early age.*
7. What age did you first engage in atypical sexual behavior*? 7 years old*
8. How has being sexually different affected your life*? Explain:*

There were a lot of judgement towards me, loss of friendships, family members distancing themselves from me.

Thank you for your help in answering these questions. Hopefully this information might be helpful to some young person dealing with their sexual orientation.

MY TRAVELING EXPERIENCE - HOMOSEXUALITY

I had the opportunity to travel around the world in March, 2020. It was a trip of a lifetime. Since I'm writing a book about Homosexuality and Transgender people; naturally these conditions stood out in my travels.

Homosexuality and Transgender people exist all over the world. The one thing that makes a difference in the open-ness of these individuals was the culture of a specific country. Some countries are very open to these people and other countries are restrictive to their open-ness.

While traveling in Egypt many years ago, one of the people in our tour group was a homosexual. He was flirting with the security guard who rode with us on the bus. The security guard was very open to his advances.

While travelling in the Fiji Islands this year (2020), the hotel where I stayed had an unusual number of homosexual males working there. Even as we traveled to a Farmer's Market, there were natives making flower arrangements. I noticed a transgender male sitting with his family wearing female clothes and make-up. Evidently this was acceptable with his family.

I asked the tour guide about the number of homosexuals and transgender people that I was seeing. He said, "what people do sexually is their business." The only restriction their country has is that they cannot marry.

BI-SEXUALITY

The pre-fix of Bi - means two. When placed in front of another word it means two of that particular thing. When placed in front of sexuality it refers to a person's sexual preference of two people (a man and a woman).

When I was 16 years old, I lived down the street of a man who was a professional dancer and a show producer. He asked me to dance in a show that he was producing. He was married and had two beautiful children. I told him he would have to ask my mother. My mother told him that I didn't know how to dance. He said that he would teach me how to dance and that he would look after me.

I worked with him on several occasions while still in high school over the years. I had the opportunity to go to several dancing schools and became proficient in dance. During that time his wife divorced him but stayed friends with him for the sake of the children.

After that time he associated with mostly male friends. I was very young and didn't know anything about bisexuality. When one is in show business you don't go around asking people about their sexuality. It's none of your business and they are not going to tell you anyway.

I did know that most of the boys or young men that were dancers were gay. We got along like brothers and sisters. They looked after me because I was so young.

I know of another young man that I have known since he was in high school who went into the service after graduation. When he came out of the service he had several male lovers. They lived together for a while and then would break up. Later he started dating a young lady. I don't think he knew which way he wanted to go.

The female bisexuals that I worked with during the summer were less obvious. One would say that they were closeted lesbians at that time. I guess because I didn't know anything about them sexually until they invited me to lunch one day. When I found out what they were into, I left. I never spoke to anyone about it.

I guess that they were bisexual because they later married men. One even had a baby, but the marriage didn't last long. The other woman stayed married until she died many years later.

As a teacher one has many students that are sexual. One student was a young lady that was attracted to females. She got pregnant at an early age while still in high school. I don't know if she was raped or whether it was consensual.

The young man that got her pregnant lived down the street from her.

Her mother and father owned several properties on the same street. They let her live in one of the houses with her young child. She had her female lovers stay with her. Together they would take care of the child until they broke up. She got pregnant again. Now she had two children, a boy, and a girl.

She did manage to graduate from high school and go on to nursing school. She continued to have her female lovers. As the years went on, she married a man and had three more children. They later got divorced.

Unless you know a person personally and are around them a lot you may not know their sexual preference. It's really none of your business unless it affects you personally.

NEWS ARTICLE ABOUT TRANSGENDER

I read an article in the *Courier Post* (a local newspaper in New Jersey) dated June 11, 2019, titled "Body + Spirit - Pink, Blue and Everything in Between". It was written by Cindy S. Handler. It was a guide to help children who are exploring their gender identity.

The article told of a North Jersey family whose child had gender issues. When the child was 16 and entered high school things changed. The child had been born a girl but wanted to be known as a boy. He changed his appearance and wanted to change his name. The family loved their child and wanted to support him with whatever decision he made. They founded out that families that didn't support their transgender people had about half of them attempt suicide.

The family found out that experts agree that many children express their gender in different ways. A minority will eventually determine that the understanding they have of their gender doesn't match the sex they were assigned at birth and choose to present a gender identity to the world that's different from their original birth certificates.

The transition may be social, through a name change, outward appearance and the pronoun they'd prefer to have used when referring to them, some will transition with help of hormones and surgery.

New Jersey is a leading force in understanding this situation. It recently became the second state, after California to require that public schools include lessons in LGBTQ history starting in 2020. Studies have indicated that similar programs drastically reduce bulling incidents at school.

The question arises as to the name they want to be known by and what bathroom they're going to use?

Informed counselors suggest:

1. That parents should listen to their child, not criticize or scold them. Support is important from both parents.
2. The child as well as the parents may benefit from seeing a therapist trained in developmental psychology.
3. Gender identity is often a "work in progress".

Sexual identity doesn't "solidify" until after puberty. The unhappiness children feel about their sex and gender identity may be due to our culture's norms that twice as many boys as girls experience unease over their gender before puberty. It may seem more acceptable for a girl to act as a Tomboy then a boy who shows interest in girl things. If children are miserable with how their gender presents themselves through the teen years, they are likely to keep feeling that way as adults.

There are several options these children have with the help of a therapist or doctors. Doctors may talk about shots to suppress their natural occurring puberty. The other way to complete the gender transition: legally. Once New Jersey residents decide to make their new identities official, they can change their birth certificates to reflect it. The Babs Siperstein Law, enacted in February, makes it easier for New Jersey residents to change the gender marker on their birth certificates. Formerly a "proof of surgery" was required, as well as certification from a professional. It also allows for a third option, in addition to male and female "X" for non-binary or undesignated.

For more information and resources in New Jersey one can go to *Garden State Equality*, garden stateequality.org; *Children's Hospital of Philadelphia Gender and Sexuality Development Clinic*, chop.edu, *Ackerman Institute Family and Gender Project* in New York City, ackerman.org; PFLAG (LGBTQ advocacy group for parents) pflag.org; *Proud Family Health* in Somerville rwjbh.org/rwj-university-hospital-somerset/treatment-care/proud–family-health//; *Institute for Personal Growth* in New Brunswick and Jersey City, ipgcounseling.com; *LGBTQ+Community Health Center* in Asbury Park, htto://prnvnacj.org/vnac-lgbtq-health-center; *Goryeb Children's Hospital* in Morristown, www.atlantichealth.org/location/hospitals/goryeb-childrens-hospital.html; GLSEN, glsen.org; HiTOP, hitops, org; *Hudson Pride Center* of New Jersey, pridecenter.org ; *Newark LGBTQ Community Center.* https://newarklgbtqcenter.org/; and the *National Center for Transgender Equality*, https://transequality.org/.